# ELEVATE

How to Level Up Every Area Of Your Life

Ellis White

# Dedication

This book is dedicated to my sister Elizabeth Anne Dodson. Thank you for being a Sister, a second Mother, and a reminder of what strength looks like. As I carry you with me in my heart for life, I hope to make you proud. Love you forever my Angel!

I also would like to dedicate this book to my parents. Ellis Sr. & Jacqueline. Thank you for believing in me and being 2 of my biggest fans.

# FORWARD

-Marcus Blandin, Founder/Ceo, Millionaires International

The word *elevate* is a word used to describe many things, but for this book elevate takes on a personal meaning of self-reflection, positioning, and rising higher to achieve optimal success.

Ellis White is a great author to write on the subject of elevation because he has been practicing his tactics to "Elevate" all of his life. He has overcome many obstacles within his personal life and has become an authority with helping others better themselves and accomplish their goals.

The strategies, tactics, and stories of perseverance Ellis share in this book are awesome. They will help you get aligned, find a healthy balance, and position yourself to be the best version of you while climbing toward your goals.

Marcus Blandin
Founder/Ceo
Millionaires International

# CHAPTER 1

*Who Are You?*

nderstanding who you are is the first step to creating the life you want. The only way to truly achieve the desires inside of your heart is to deeply know and understand yourself and the things that are important to you. Getting yourself aligned and in tune with your values and morals can help to establish a strong foundation for success. Even for those of us who feel we truly know ourselves well, it is important to give ourselves a good tune-up to make sure we are on the right track and maintain optimal efficiency as you move toward your goals.

By simply being in tune with yourself, you will increase your happiness, lessen internal conflicts, improve your decision-making skills, boost your self-control, become more resistant to social pressure, better empathize with others, and give yourself ultimate pleasure. Knowing yourself makes your feel MORE ALIVE!

Life is meant to be lived to the fullest, but to accomplish that, one must know himself deeply. A true understanding of the self does not end with knowing one's strengths or pleasures. One must know his or her weaknesses and fears. The human brain is like a large computer; it requires regular assessment and maintenance. To live life to the fullest, one must assess and reassess themselves to learn what triggers feelings of happiness and fulfillment and what triggers feelings of sadness and defeat. By understanding what brings on those feelings, it becomes easier to maintain your overall happiness. In this book, we will dive into you and look into what shapes your world.

"To know thyself is the beginning of Wisdom."

- Socrates

With that said, I am grateful and honored to share the exact process that I have used to help thousands of people take their lives to the Next Level. These tactics have helped them achieve their maximum potential and actualize their deepest desires.

It is Time to Elevate.

**<u>Elevation Exercise</u>**

*Answer the following questions. Make sure to WRITE YOUR ANSWERS DOWN!*

*1.) What are my strengths?*

*2.) What are my weaknesses?*

*3.) Where are there opportunities for me to improve?*

*4.) What threatens my growth the most?*

# CHAPTER 2

*Be A Dreamer*

We are all born dreamers; nevertheless, our environment has a way of putting a little fog in our dreams, making it difficult to navigate them. The things you experience and give energy to can impact your dreams and the way that you see yourself. If you are not careful, you will end up settling for less than what you truly deserve. This is why most people never reach their full potential to create and live out their dreams.

Everything around us has the potential to shape our lives, so while we might not always be able to control everything, it is important that we are selective of what we allow close enough to influence us. Now, that may be easier said than done, but with practice, consistency, and persistence, it can be achieved. Dreams are just figments of your imagination that you have not yet brought into full fruition. Turning dreams into reality takes some work, but it also makes for a great reward when finally accomplished.

*The Dream*

I can remember as a kid having this dream of being a successful businessman. I watched my father leave every morning in suits and dress clothes. I watched him take business calls and I watched him close deals. This made me want to do the same. So, I talked my parents into letting me play with an old briefcase and I would walk around my home pretending to be a "successful businessman." I would dress up in my church clothes, answer imaginary business calls on our house phone, and use monopoly money for fake transactions. I even got my parents to play along with me. I had a Dream. There was no way you could tell me that I wasn't a successful businessman.

As I grew older, I lost track of that dream. LIFE started throwing curveballs my way and as we all know, when life kicks in, anything can happen. Even worse, I started allowing my environment and the people around me to influence my dreams. I let FEAR alter my vision, and of course, without vision, we are moving in the blind. The following are several Fears that many people allow to handicap them:

- Fear of Failure

- Fear of being Judged/Overwhelming Desire to be Accepted

- Fear of Change

- Fear of Success


The moment I stopped letting Fear dictate my actions, life as I knew it changed. No longer was I going through life passively settling for less. I transformed my dreams into a vision and that vision eventually became my reality. I began to feel empowered and confident that my dreams were obtainable. This was the moment of truth. It was the shift that desperately needed to happen so that I could start to become that successful businessman I had always dreamed of being.

I came to realize that Fear was the culprit that had been holding me back the entire time. We must eliminate Fear from our lives at all cost. The more I thought about Fear, the better I understood that it was *False Evidence Appearing Real*. It was not truly real, but I was giving it power over my dreams and over me. FEAR is the number one DREAM KILLER.

### *Elevation Exercise*

*Close your eyes and dream. What does your perfect life look like? Be as specific and detailed as possible. Write down some of the great things you see. Now list your Fears. Write down how you can overcome every last one of them!*

# CHAPTER 3

*Life Is A Gift: The Paradigm Shift*

You can get rid of the "Poor Me" mentality. Life isn't happening to you, it's happening for you. Your struggles show how strong you are. They are tests meant to challenge you into achieving your dreams and living the life you have always dreamed of.

So many people allow their struggles to define the quality of their lives. This cannot be the case if you are looking to escape the status of "average." The best lessons come as a result of our failures. In those moments, we learn what will hinder us and what has the potential to propel us along the journey to success. Yes, there is some pain in struggling and pain in what we perceive to be failure. But you cannot truly appreciate the pleasure of Victory without ever have suffered from a type loss. A loss does not mean you have failed as long as you choose to learn from your mistakes. You have only truly failed when you decide to give up and quit. That is when all forward progress has come to a complete halt.

For this reason, we must relentlessly pursue our dreams. We must stop allowing the pain of our experiences to negatively shape our belief systems. Our thoughts and beliefs become our reality. How you choose to think of something directly affects the outcome. Instead of believing you are getting the short end of the stick, you must believe that you are preparing for your glorious victory.

Actively shifting your way of thinking in this way is a Paradigm Shift – the essential moment that allows you to turn your fears and pains into momentum that will carry you to success. You are the author of your own story and it is up to you to decide how to narrate it. There will be many moments in life which can inspire a Paradigm Shift, but in order to recognize and receive it, it is essential to be in the right mindset. Being open and receptive is what will allow you to prepare for constant change and elevating toward your dreams.

Similarly, you must recognize that you can either be the victim or the hero of your story and "write" it with this in mind. Circumstances that life throws your way can either empower you or it can derail you entirely based on the way you perceive them. Do not be the person who only focuses on the negative in every situation when there are opportunities to see it in the positive. What you choose to focus on will become the dictator of your desires. Maintaining a positive and focused mindset will plant seeds of success in line with your dreams, keeping you in tune to your goals and desires. Misconceptions mixed with a pessimistic mindset can create a Negative Shift that leads to your conscious mind planting the wrong type of seeds.

### *Elevation Exercise*

*Think of three difficult situations you have had to face in the last three months. Did you respond negatively or positively? Write down how you reacted and try to see the ways in which you could have handled the situation differently. What could you have done better? What actions could you have taken to encourage a positive Paradigm Shift?*

# CHAPTER 4

*Passion: The Internal Flame That Burns*

Passion is the fire that fuels creative expression, areas of extreme interest, and drives adventurous curiosity. Society tells us to go to school, find a job, get married, have kids, etc.

This is GREAT! …

If you are passionate about accomplishing those things. If you are not, then you have been encouraged to follow a blueprint that was never meant for you. You must identify what you are passionate about. Passion is not about money or some type of material compensation. It is not doing something just because you have to. It is not following someone else's dreams. Passion is about feeling good internally. It is doing what you love to do.

Living a life filled with passion gives you a sense of empowerment and confidence. It helps to create the life we truly desire. How can someone be truly happy if every day they waste life doing something they care nothing about? If you go through every day merely existing, you are wasting precious time that could be used to help you evolve into the person of your dreams. So, ask yourself, are you merely existing or are you living the life you envisioned for yourself in your dreams?

If not, what are you waiting for?

Analyze your life up until this point and try to figure out where you may have lost or allowed your flame to be dimmed. Have there been moments where someone or something dimmed your flame? Did something happen that caused you to dim your shine yourself and stray from the path that leads to your happiness? Are you creating your own path or are you just following the road that others have built for themselves?

Never let anyone or anything put out your fire. Let your flame of passion burn bright. From today forward, fuel your fire so that it burns hotter and brighter than ever before.

### *Elevation Exercise*

*-What are you passionate about?*

*- How does it relate to your dreams?*

*- What are three things you can do over the next thirty days to get you closer to your dreams?*

# CHAPTER 5

*Purpose: The Feeling of Fulfillment*

Now that you have identified what you are passionate about, you can start to define your purpose. Purpose is something that I have found people really struggle with. Whether it's discovering their purpose or defining what it means to live a life full of purpose, it can be difficult to find the answers you are looking for. With the help of your Passion, your Purpose should be clearer.

Purpose is usually derived from personal experiences that help to shape and mold the essence of who you are. This life-defining experience is most often linked to painful or pleasurable moments in life, but both are valid and, when properly identified, can lead to amazing things.

The darkest point in my life is characterized by a full-blown depression. It impacted every area of my life. There was a point where the only thing I had the strength to do was sleep. I couldn't face what my life had become. With tears running down my face, I would beg God for my internal pain to go away. I was clueless and lost. I had no direction and I had no hope.

One day, I decided that I no longer wanted to feel this way – weak, out of control, inadequate, and like a complete failure. It just was not going to work for me anymore. I decided to put my life back together, piece by piece. My mindset was the first to change. With the momentum that sprung from my Paradigm Shift, my physical health was next on the list. As my routines changed, I started to love myself again. I gained access to the power that I always possessed inside. These decisions and actions literally changed my life! I tell you this so that you can understand how your decisions and actions can change your life as well.

During this struggle, I felt like a victim, but now I know that I desperately needed that experience. All the pain I experienced was shaping me into the person I needed to become: a person whose Purpose is to help those who have been through similar experiences as mine regain their confidence and empower them to live their best lives. In the midst of all of that pain, I found my Purpose. The darkness I experienced at that point in my life shaped me into the purpose-driven powerhouse I am today. My Passion and my Purpose is to help people better the quality of their lives.

I thought of my Purpose as a piece of me. But as with many other things, just because I possessed it, that didn't mean I knew how to channel it to fulfill my dreams. I did not yet fully understand what my Purpose could do.

After discovering my Purpose, I channeled it all into real estate. Once in the business, I was not your traditional agent; I actively strove to help those in need. I quickly joined a real estate program called "Help" which taught people how to short sale, prevent foreclosure, and transition from a home under any kind of duress.

During my time in real estate, I also decided to open a training company. Instinctively, I understood that I didn't want to own just another "gym" or "bootcamp." So, I made sure that I stayed clear of the traditional "high-five, workout, go home" model. My interest was not only in helping people improve their physical strength, but in helping them improve their mental and emotional strength I want to help people them transform into the who they desire to be and live the lives they deserve.

Helping people gives me an immense feeling of fulfillment. I discovered that my Purpose is not just a piece of me, but who I naturally am – who I was destined to be.

When you contemplate and consider your Purpose, connect with who you are and how you feel. Does the thought of fulfilling that purpose fill you with a sense of euphoria? Your Purpose should be fulfilling. It is often defined as **the one thing you would do even if you were not compensated.**

# CHAPTER 6

*Power: It Can Create or It Can Destroy*

No one can gift you power. You have always owned your own power. However, we often forget how much power we actually possess. The capacity to become empowered, to change, to self-elevate, and more, has always been embedded within each of us.

One of our most important powers is decision-making. Usually, decisions are based on our beliefs. Deciding what you will focus on, what actions you will take, and what things and experiences mean to you are vital to your success. All these decisions have the power to create and shape your destiny.

Allowing yourself to focus on the negative in life will only serve to destroy your dreams. When you give negativity all of your power, it tends to spread into multiple aspects of your life. Negativity can leave you feeling as though you are completely drained – completely powerless. Negative situations and thoughts have the potential to draw from your energy, but ultimately, the power is yours. Take control so that the negativity does not cause a permanent power outage.

To tap into your true self-serving power, you must switch your focus to the positive. You must make sure that your beliefs are in alignment with your desires. You cannot believe you are worthless and live a life full of purpose. As long as your beliefs stem from feelings of inadequacy or worthlessness, all of the decisions and actions that follow will be tainted. This is why you must use your power to "CHANGE YOUR STORY!" Allow positive thoughts and desires to fuel you and be your power core. Too many negative or limiting beliefs will be absolutely detrimental to this power core. The world around us already provides enough darkness and negativity to smother your light, so you must actively filter what is allowed in your subconscious where limiting beliefs get stored and dreams go to die.

Your TRUE POWER will be on full display once you learn to adapt your thinking to see everything from a helpful or positive vantage point. Exercising and learning how to utilize this power creates the life you truly want!

# CHAPTER 7

*Identify Your Imbalance: No Balance. No Peace*

Now that you have solidified a stable foundation for growth, it is time to focus on taking your life to the Next Level.

When growing, improving, and enhancing life, it is important to maintain balance. Your emotional and spiritual being, physical health, relationships, and your finances will all need special attention along the journey to your dream life. These elements are all connected and life can spiral downward quickly and suddeny if they are not taken into consideration.

An imbalance in any of the aforementioned areas can create high levels of stress and severely impact all of your progress. By placing focus on these areas through daily action, you will be able to create the reality that you have envisioned for yourself. Your reality is shaped entirely by your thoughts. Your thoughts are usually influenced by your mood and emotions. The best decision you can make for yourself is to constantly work on controlling your emotions and attempting to be in the best mood possible. This will help keep you balanced and on the right track. Balance leads to peace, so creating balance between your business, finance, and health should be high on your priority list.

Finances can affect all of the other areas that were mentioned above because most people place a lot of importance on this element of their lives. When someone's finances are out of whack, it creates immense emotional distress, which often leads to negative impacts on their physical well-being. It can also cause rifts and tension in romantic and platonic relationships seeing as financial instability triggers many arguments.

This is why identifying your imbalances is so important. The disruption of your peace is not something to be taken lightly and should be protected whenever possible. Without balance, there cannot be peace. Imbalance will hinder your elevation in all areas.

## Elevation Exercise

*Write a list and honestly rate each of the following with a score of between 1 and 10. After rating, write at least one thing that you can change to help improve your health in that element.*

*- Financial Health*

*- Spiritual Health*

*- Emotional Health*

*- Physical Health*

# CHAPTER 8

*Master Your Emotions and Stay
Spiritually Connected*

**L**ET'S BE HONEST! WE ARE ALL EMOTIONAL!! This is not a weakness. Most instinctual actions are driven by emotions whether negative or positive. Subsequently, virtually everything we do is informed by and in order to impact our current emotional state. While our overall goal is always to search for happiness, that doesn't always go as planned. Most of our lives are emotional rollercoasters because there are outside forces that are sometimes beyond our control. Things like work, kids, family, friends, and even social media can and do influence our emotions. This is why we must keep a strong spiritual connection based on individual belief systems.

Take, for example, the famous question, "What is your why?" The answer to this question is usually connected to how you want to feel after you have achieved your desired outcome. It is also usually connected to your spirituality and purpose.

A good practice or method to stay connected is journaling. Journaling is a powerful way to maintain a connection to how you are feeling and a great way to track your ups and downs. This is a way to also see where you need to make improvements on how you perceive and react to things. You want to use your journal to identify the emotions and feelings that serve you and become more resilient to the ones that do not.

This will lead to an improved sense of self-awareness. Through self-awareness, you will learn to maintain a positive mindset that will help you focus on what truly matters: Your Dream. Do not allow yourself to wander back into a state that will regress the growth and progress you have already made. It can be very easy and tempting to revert back into a negative state of mind, but once you have identified the patterns in your life that lead to a negative spiral and learn to concentrate on your purpose, you will be able to successfully reorient yourself on the most expeditious path to accomplishing your goals. The best mindset is one where you are totally focused and in full awareness of all the things around you that can impact your way of thinking or feeling. If you can identify what has happened when you feel you have taken a step backwards, you will be able to master the art of self-realignment, keep your concentration intact, and accomplish all things in life that you have set out to do.

Understanding your emotions better will keep you aligned with your core values and help you stay grounded spiritually. Your spirit is the root of your genuine character and is an important factor in being able to love yourself for who you genuinely are.

### _Elevation Exercise_

_Think of the last three days. How would you describe each day overall? Did your decisions and activities for that day align with your core values? If not, what could you have done differently?_

# CHAPTER 9

*Health Is Wealth*

You can achieve a high level of financial success and still be unhappy due to your physical and emotional states. Introducing practices to keep your physical health in check is just as important as keeping your finances in check. Can you imagine achieving every financial goal you ever dreamed of but not even being healthy enough to enjoy it?

Are you waking up feeling energized and ready to conquer the day, or are you struggling to find the energy to even get out of bed? Are you bothered by high levels of activity? Do you resent the fatigue that you always seem to carry with you from the day before? All of these and more are definite signs of physical imbalance. With issues like heart disease, diabetes, and cancer being so prevalent and pervasive, it is important that you take complete control over your lifestyle and monitor your health accordingly to minimize you risk for these illnesses. Being physically active is essential, but what you eat and how you eat it are equally as important. You cannot continue to cram junk into your body and expect to feel like anything other than a piece of junk. What you eat and fuel your body with has a direct effect on your physique and on your energy levels. Too much junk will make your engine sluggish.

A good practice is to live an active lifestyle. Doing so not only helps boost your energy levels, but it also helps manage stress levels and helps improve your confidence and self-esteem. Taking control of your lifestyle ensures that you look good and feel good. It reminds you daily that you have the power and self-control to dictate your outcomes.

# CHAPTER 10

*Relationships Are Key*

Who you spend time with does matter! Romantic, familial, business, and all other social relationships all help shape and influence your success. Look at the people that you spend the most time with and it will usually be a reflection of who you are. However, it is a common misconception that these external relationships hold a bigger impact on you than the internal relationship you keep with yourself. You spend the most time with yourself! So, having a healthy relationship with the self is the most important and beneficial relationship you can have. Understanding yourself helps keep you in-line with your goals, keeps you motivated, allows you to work toward your Purpose, and it affects every other relationship you have. You are able to have a deeper and more meaningful connection with others because you have a deep and meaningful relationship with yourself and a clinical understanding of your core values and what shapes you.

Relationships are not one-way streets. Often, the focus is on what you can get out of a relationship instead of what you might be able to give or contribute. A good way to strengthen the relationships you currently have is to begin a process of Daily Deposits. Daily Deposits are intentional investments into the relationships that mean the most to you on a daily basis. A deposit can be as simple as telling a family member that you enjoy their company or that you love them. By showing your love, honor, respect, and appreciation for others, you automatically increase the strength of that relationship and encourage it to grow. Additionally, by doing this you will also be making Daily Deposits to yourself. It is important to understand that by increasing the value that you add to a relationship, the more you will receive from it in return. As the old adage goes: The more you give, the more you shall receive. By sharing your genuine thoughts and appreciation for others, you begin to unlock the best and most amazing parts of you.

To be clear, this does not mean that you must give your entire self to others and let yourself be taken advantage of or undervalued. Relationships like this are incredibly toxic and can debilitate any and all progress you have made. If a relationship has become toxic, it is extremely important that you remove yourself from it immediately. Often, that is easier said than done, but it is a necessity for growth and for maintaining a healthy emotional and mental state. Sometimes, the toxicity in a relationship doesn't come from the other person, but from YOU. Being negative-minded is a good indicator of toxicity. Negative-minded people pull others down and if that negative-minded person is you, you will be pulling yourself down as well as everyone else around you. Contrastingly, positive-minded people pull and elevate others around them. In moments of darkness, they will help stop you from completely sabotaging your own success. If you are falling into these habits, make sure to re-evaluate your mindset.

The best thing about relationships is that by investing in them, you are able to help others. Great relationships can be a valuable asset to your growth and elevation. For example, in business, cultivating healthy relationships can be the difference between a successful deal and a deal gone bad. It is dependent on whether or not both parties bring value to the relationship. While there are times where it may not be possible, keep in mind that your goal for every situation in a relationship is to have a win-win resolution.

The tips in this chapter are helpful for improving any and all kinds of relationships you currently have or hope to build.

# CHAPTER 11

*Visualize & Believe: Keep the Faith*

I t is time to make sure that your vision is Clear. Do you believe in your vision? Do you trust that you can accomplish your dream? Do you believe?

Find somewhere you can be alone, where it is peaceful and quiet. Now, envision the life you want. Close your eyes and paint the masterpiece. Yes, utilize your faith and belief systems to get in tune with the life you envision. To paint your masterpiece, you must visualize and fully believe that it is obtainable. This life is real and it is yours. You must stay connected to it and fine-tune the details each step of the way.

Over time, the belief in dreams might start to diminish. The ways of the world and the negativity within it can be a huge distraction and weigh heavily on belief systems. That can also lead to questioning the attainability of dreams and one's capacity to accomplish goals. The most destructive issue that plagues anyone's ability to accomplish his or her dream is to believe that it is not attainable. If you do not have a clear understanding of your dreams now, the details (and more) will fade when difficult situations arise. To accomplish and achieve your dream, your vision must remain sharp and your focus, solid. If you get off track, make sure to take the necessary steps and time needed to get yourself back on track. Do NOT let a small setback derail you from your path. During these moments, your faith plays a large role. Begin to think about the time you have spent working toward your dreams and how far you have truly come. Think of the many reasons why your dream arose in the first place. What value will achieving your dream bring to your life? This should help you reorient yourself if you need it. In the midst of the world's negativity, please do not become your own worst enemy. Do not sabotage your own dream. Evaluate your situation and use logic to respond to a situation, not just your emotions. Often, the best way to guarantee your success is through soulsearching and introspection. This will help you think and can even help you discover things that have potentially been standing in your way. Remember, the way that we think about setbacks and "failures" plays a large role in our overall mood, mindset, and ability to succeed.

Believing in and invoking the phrase "I can do anything!" is a positive affirmation that will keep you from self-sabotage. Belief in yourself is fundamental for your success. In the event that you slip up, and find it difficult to believe in yourself, your faith, and your beliefs, take a moment to look inward and refer back to your plan while stating (with enthusiasm) your positive affirmation. This is one of the benefits to having a plan and writing it down; you are able to backtrack to see exactly where you might have been wrong, see where you can improve, and get an overall better idea of the challenge at hand.

Along your journey, there will be challenges, but you must keep the Faith. Remember that when there is change, there will be discomfort. BELIEVE. Believe that you are in control. Believe in your power. Believe that you CAN obtain the life you have envisioned.

*Fruition*

I often remember the time I spent looking for a location to open my first transformation center. After painstakingly reviewing my options, I finally submitted an application. I was... denied. This wasn't supposed to happen. This was not how I planned it! Instead of immediately trying again, I went back to running my transformation center out of a local park. I had reached a moment that threatened to break me back down to where I started. I found myself questioning whether or not this was all worth it and whether or not I was doing the right thing. When I realized just how much I had sunken into my old habits of doubting myself, I immediately set out to cancel those thoughts. I focused on my Dream. I focused on my Vision. I regained my Power and Faith in myself. The third location I found approved me under better terms than I could have ever imagined or gotten from the locations I was denied from. If I would have given up, I would not be where I am today. I would not be able to write this book today.

The moral of this story: BELIEVE AND KEEP THE FAITH and no one and nothing will be able to stop you.

# CHAPTER 12

*Strategy & Execution: The Imple-
mentation of Your Dreams*

*"Without strategy, execution is aimless. Without Execution Strategy is useless."*

*- Morris Chang, CEO TSMC*

ou have your vision. Now you must create a game plan and execute.

This plan is going to be your road map to achieving your dreams. Without a game plan, even the idea of achieving your dreams can seem overwhelming. There is nothing worse than knowing exactly what you need to do but having no idea how to get it done. This happens to everyone more often than you would think. Everyone has had that moment of extreme stress where they berate themselves with the extremely long list of things that need to get done. "I need to do this, and that, and that...!" The pressure and the long, unorganized, daunting list becomes impossible to complete. Instead of taking this approach and trying to focus on all of the things you have to do, focus on only one action that will move you a step closer to your goal. This strategy allows you to maximize your energy output and ultimately dramatically improves the likelihood of you getting things done. By moving methodically and taking one step at a time, you remove the overwhelming anxiety and stress from taking action and executing your plan. Move one step at a time and build the dream one brick at a time.

Once you have executed the first step, there will be a feeling of accomplishment. Allow yourself to celebrate this victory. There is never a win too small to be celebrated! Continue with this method and before you know it, you'll accomplish the things on your list. That feeling of successfully moving in the direction of your dreams is addicting. You will find yourself making moves without overthinking because of the confidence that comes with accomplishing the things you set out to do. With confidence, it becomes even easier to create and follow a strategy. Now, you are properly oriented; you are facing the direction of all you have ever wanted and worked for. You are well on your way to accomplishing and building your Dream.

Smile. You're getting closer.

Take (continuous) action using the tools provided and watch as your life flourishes.

I am confident in this process, because I went from the kid who was contemplating life and struggling to make a living, to a person who helped thousands of people transform their lives, created a business that has made millions of dollars, and now living the life I always dreamed of. Even this book was a part of my dreams.

If I can do it, You can too!

It's time to ELEVATE. You are ready.

# ABOUT THE AUTHOR

Ellis White
www.elliswhitejr.com

Ellis White Jr. is the owner of Premier Fitness & Performance LLC., President of Premier Cares (non-Profit 501 c3), Co-Owner of Woman on Fire, and a Motivational Speaker.

Ellis graduated with honors from the University of Central Oklahoma with a B.B.A in Business Management. While in college, he joined the local Omega Psi Phi Fraternity Inc. chapter (Sigma Kappa). He also has a Real Estate license with multiple designations, is a Nike Certified trainer, and has an International Sports Science Association Certification in Personal Training.

Ellis was born and raised in Carson, California. He is dedicated to improving his community and anyone who crosses his path. His mission is to help people live confidently, stimulate constant improvement in mental and physical strength, and ultimately upgrade their overall quality of life. When he is not actively engaging in doing his best super-hero performance, he is spending priceless time with his family; his beautiful wife and their two handsome boys.


FOR BOOKING OR SPEAKING EVENTS PLEASE
CONTACT US AT


**WWW.ELLISWHITEJR.COM**